Jimmy Carter

 Community BUILDERS

Builder of Peace

by
Linda and
Charles
George

Children's Press®
A Division of Grolier Publishing
New York / London / Hong Kong / Sydney
Danbury, Connecticut

Photo Credits

Photographs ©: AP/Wide World Photos: 8 (Horace Cort), 31 (Bob Daugherty), 32 (Wilson), 15, 16, 18, 25 center, 28, 29, 34; Archive Photos: 38 (Corinne Dufka/Reuters), back cover (Steve Jaffe/Reuters), 2 (Mike Theiler/Reuters), 12, 17, 19, 24, 26; Corbis-Bettmann: 6, 9 (AFP), 40 (Robert Maass), 25 top (Wally McNamee), 3 (Joseph Sohm/ChromoSohm, Inc.), 10, 23, 35 (UPI), 25 bottom; Jimmy Carter National Historic Site: 13; Liaison Agency, Inc.: cover (William Coupon), 43 (Gifford); NDI/Carter Center: 37 (Yuriah Tanzil); PhotoEdit: 44 (Tony Freeman); Sygma: 20 (Arthur Grace).

Visit Children's Press on the Internet at:
http://publishing.grolier.com

Library of Congress Cataloging-in-Publication Data

George, Linda.
    Jimmy Carter : builder of peace / by Linda and Charles George.
        p. cm. — (Community builders)
    Includes bibliographical references (p.) and index.
    Summary: Presents a biography of United States president, from his childhood in Georgia to his current activities with the Carter Center and Habitat for Humanity, discussing important historical events that happened during his career.
    ISBN: 0-516-21601-5 (lib. bdg.)
    1. Carter, Jimmy, 1924– —Juvenile literature. 2. Presidents—United States—Biography—Juvenile literature. [1. Carter, Jimmy, 1924– 2. Presidents.] I. George, Charles 1949– . II. Title. III. Series.
E873.G46   2000
973.926'092—dc21
[B]   99-087720

©2000 Children's Press®, a Division of Grolier Publishing Co., Inc.
Printed in the United States of America.
1 2 3 4 5 6 7 8 9 10 R 09 08 07 06 05 04 03 02 01 00

Contents

Jimmy delivers a speech on poverty in the world in Olso, Norway.

Chapter ONE

Stand Up for What Is Right

Has anyone ever asked you to do something you knew was wrong? Were you brave enough to stand up to them and tell them "No"? Have you ever seen someone younger than you being picked on by a bully? Did you help them stand up for themselves?

One man who knows about standing up for what is right is Jimmy Carter, the thirty-ninth president of the United States. He grew up on a farm in Georgia in the 1920s, when not many white people treated African-Americans as equals. Many of Jimmy's friends were African-American, and he stood up for them, even when he was criticized for it.

Racial Segregation

From the late 1800s until the 1960s, African-Americans and white people were segregated by law in the United States, especially in the South. Segregation means the separation of groups of people because of their race, religion, or culture. A series of new laws, passed in the 1960s, ended racial segregation in the United States.

Because of segregation, African-Americans had to sit in separate areas from white people in movie theaters, restaurants, and on buses.

As governor of Georgia and as president of the United States, Jimmy stood up for everyone—rich or poor, black or white, male or female. Sometimes what he did wasn't popular, but he always believed that what he was doing was right.

Now that Jimmy Carter is no longer the president, he still helps people all over the world. He helps

Jimmy Carter won the Presidential Medal of Freedom in 1999.

them build their homes, find food and water, and fight diseases.

Jimmy Carter has spent his life standing up for what he believes. You can be brave and stand up for what's right, too.

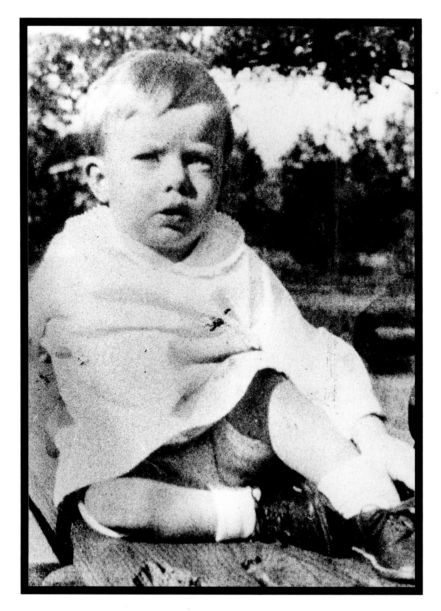

Jimmy at one year old

Chapter TWO

Georgia Roots Run Deep

James Earl Carter, Jr., was born in the small town of Plains, Georgia, on October 1, 1924. His parents called him "Jimmy." They never dreamed he would grow up to be president of the United States.

Jimmy grew up on his parents' farm in Archery, a small community near Plains. The Carter home had no electricity and no running water. Their bathroom was a small shed, or outhouse, behind the house. The Carters hand-pumped water from a well in the yard.

Jimmy's Parents

Jimmy's parents,
Lillian and Earl Carter

Jimmy's father, James Earl Carter, Sr., was well respected, and considered a natural leader by the community. He was a farmer, merchant, Sunday-school teacher, and school-board member.

His mother, Lillian Gordy Carter, "Miss Lillian," was a hard-working registered nurse. Miss Lillian taught her children that all people are equal and should be treated the same. This was unusual for a southerner in the days before the Civil Rights Movement, when African-Americans and white people were kept separate. In those days, many whites thought that they were better than blacks.

**Jimmy and his family moved into this farmhouse
when Jimmy was four years old.**

Everyone in the family worked on the farm
from sunrise until sunset. They had no farm machin-
ery, so all of the plowing was done with mules. They
chopped wood for cooking and for heat in winter.

When he had finished his chores, Jimmy earned
his own spending money. At the age of five, he sold
boiled peanuts on the streets of Plains. When he was
nine, he bought five big bales of cotton. He stored

Plains, Georgia

Plains is a small town in southwestern Georgia. When Jimmy Carter was born, Plains had a population of 683 people. Today, it is home to 716 people. Every September, the community holds its annual Peanut Festival, which includes a parade, arts and crafts, performances, peanut museum, peanut education, peanut farming equipment, and exhibits.

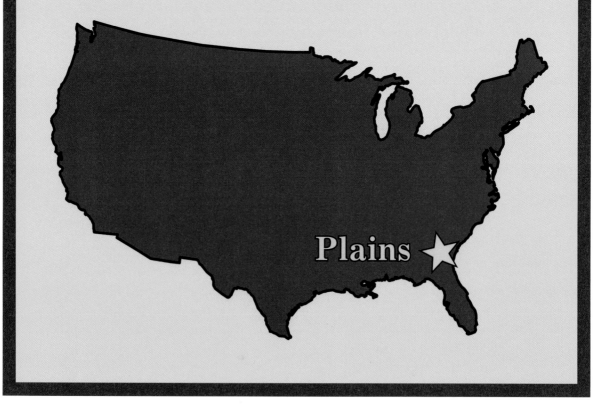

Plains

them for a few years until the price of cotton had tripled, then sold them for a nice profit.

Growing up in rural Georgia helped shape Jimmy's character. He respected his parents. The Carter family attended church every Sunday. At home, Earl Carter's word was law. He alone made all the family decisions. Jimmy, his sisters (Gloria and Ruth), and his brother (Billy) obeyed their father without question. Jimmy accepted his father's way of running the family as the correct way.

Jimmy's father, Earl, stands behind Jimmy and his sisters, Gloria and Ruth.

Jimmy at his graduation from the U.S. Naval Academy, with his future wife Rosalynn and his mother, Lillian

Jimmy attended the Plains public schools. For a sixth-grade assignment, he wrote a list of "healthy mental attitudes" (or qualities to guide your life). On this list, he included, "the habit of expecting to accomplish what you attempt," which means to keep trying until you succeed. This became a lifelong habit of his. Jimmy graduated from Plains High School in 1941. After high school, he attended Georgia Southwestern College and the Georgia

Institute of Technology. Jimmy had always wanted to join the navy. His dream came true in 1942, when he was appointed to the United States Naval Academy in Annapolis, Maryland. This is the school that trains young people to become officers in the United States Navy.

In 1945, Jimmy asked Rosalynn Smith to go with him to a movie. That first date made a big impression on him. Jimmy told his mother that night, "She's the girl I'm going to marry." Jimmy and Rosalynn married on July 7, 1946, a month after he had graduated from the Naval Academy with a bachelor of science degree.

Jimmy and Rosalynn Carter leaving their wedding reception in Plains, Georgia

17

Rosalynn and the Children

Rosalynn Smith was born in Plains on August 18, 1927. She was the best friend of Jimmy's sister Ruth. After they were married, Jimmy and Rosalynn had three sons and one daughter. John William "Jack" Carter was born in 1947. James Earl "Chip" Carter III was born in 1950. Donnel Jeffrey "Jeff" Carter was born in 1952. In 1967, their daughter, Amy Lynn, was born.

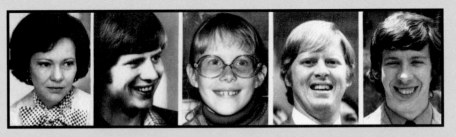

Rosalynn and the Carters' four children:
Chip, Amy, Jack, and Jeff

Jimmy loved being in the navy. He served on both the Atlantic and the Pacific oceans. Admiral Hyman Rickover assigned Jimmy to help build the nuclear submarine *Sea Wolf.* Lieutenant Carter seemed to be on his way to becoming an admiral. But something happened in 1953 that changed his life forever.

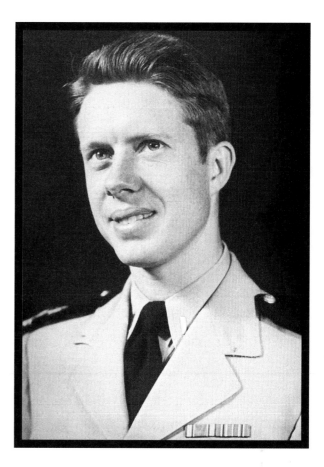

**Carter in his navy
uniform in 1948**

Jimmy learned that his father was very ill. He went to Plains to be with his father. Many people visited the Carter home to pay their respects and to tell Earl good-bye. Everyone who came by wanted to thank Earl for helping them and their families.

Jimmy and Rosalynn Carter

When his father died, Jimmy thought a lot about all the wonderful things people had said about Earl. And he thought about his own life. He decided to leave the navy and move back to Plains. Rosalynn wanted Jimmy to stay in the navy, but his mind was made up. They moved to Plains, and he took over the family peanut business in the winter of 1953.

Even though Jimmy and Rosalynn had saved some money, hard times awaited them in Plains. Many people owed money to Earl's business, but they couldn't pay. Jimmy had to find a way to earn money to support his family. He sold fertilizer and seed peanuts to local farmers and used the money to buy the crops the farmers harvested. Then he resold the crops for a profit.

Jimmy discovered he couldn't run the business alone. Rosalynn helped by doing the company's bookkeeping (paying the bills and keeping track of the money). After a few years, they became equal partners in the business. From then on, Jimmy never made a decision without talking to Rosalynn first. They were a team.

Chapter THREE

Running for Office

Following his father's example, Jimmy Carter wanted to help others, and he thought that politics would be the best way to accomplish this goal. In 1962, Carter decided to run for the Georgia State Senate. He worked hard to get people to vote for him. The hard work paid off. He won!

Carter served four years in the Georgia Senate. He helped improve patient care in mental hospitals, and helped pass laws to prevent dishonest elections. Most of all, Carter looked for ways to save money for Georgia taxpayers and to improve their living conditions.

Jimmy and Rosalynn Carter during Jimmy's unsuccessful campaign for governor of Georgia in 1966

In 1966, Carter decided to run for governor. He lost that election but didn't lose his dream. He kept campaigning until the 1970 election. He wanted everyone to know who he was and what he wanted to do for Georgians.

During the long four years of campaigning, Carter delivered almost two thousand speeches and shook hands with more than a half million people. Once, in a crowd of people, he accidentally shook hands with a clothing store dummy! Everyone laughed, including Carter. He told one of his helpers, "Give her a brochure!"

In 1970, Carter was elected governor of Georgia. He looked for ways the state could save money. He put a herd of cattle on the lawn of a state hospital so the grass wouldn't have to be mowed. Money saved on mowing was used to improve patient care. Carter helped to reform prisons and

Carter is all smiles on election night in 1970.

improve schools. He worked to protect Georgia's environment, natural resources, and historic sites.

Considering all of the good he had done for the people of Georgia, Jimmy Carter might have decided that being governor was enough. But he wanted to do more. He wanted to help the whole country. In 1972, he decided to run for president of the United States.

24

The President's Job

The president of the United States is the head of the executive branch of the government. He

also serves as the commander-in-chief of the armed forces. He can propose new laws. The president performs ceremonial duties such as entertaining foreign leaders and hosting state dinners. He also negotiates and signs treaties with other countries.

As president, Carter oversaw the military, met with foreign leaders, and signed treaties with other nations.

Carter visits with factory workers in New Hampshire during the 1976 presidential campaign.

To win the election, Carter had to make himself known to people across the United States. Outside Georgia, though, no one knew him. When they heard that Jimmy Carter was running for president, many people asked, "Jimmy who?"

That changed as he campaigned all over the country. He and Rosalynn spoke to thousands of people. Carter told them, "If I become president, you may not always agree with what I do. I cannot promise that I'll always be right. I can promise that I'll never be satisfied with less than the best."

People listened, and they liked what they heard. In 1976, Jimmy won the Democratic Party's nomination for president of the United States. Walter Mondale, a senator from Minnesota, became his vice-presidential running mate.

A Different Kind of Candidate

While campaigning, Carter carried his own suitcases and stayed in private homes rather than in hotels. He wanted to meet the people of the United States. He even fixed a tear in his jacket instead of asking someone to do it for him.

Sometimes he wore jeans and T-shirts instead of suits and ties. People could see he was a regular person.

Chapter FOUR

His Days at the White House

Carter with some of his family on Election Day, November 2, 1976

On November 2, 1976, Jimmy Carter was elected the thirty-ninth president of the United States. More than 150,000 people attended his inauguration in Washington, D.C.—the ceremony in which he took the oath of office. Rosalynn, the new First Lady, stood at his side as he promised to uphold the Constitution of the United States.

28

**The Carters' famous walk down Pennsylvania Avenue
to the White House after the inauguration**

After his speech, Carter did something no other newly elected president had ever done. Instead of riding in a limousine down Pennsylvania Avenue to the White House, he and his family walked the entire 1½ miles (2.4 kilometers). The crowd cheered for their new president!

Carter once said, "Every day gone is a day wasted if you haven't crammed in every single bit of accomplishment you can." He began his presidency with a long list of things he wanted to accomplish. His goals involved lowering taxes, cutting government spending, and creating jobs. He also wanted to make it easier for people to get good health care. Knowing that people feared nuclear war, Carter wanted to reduce the number of nuclear weapons in the world. He also wanted people in other countries to have more freedom.

Carter proposed an energy bill. He wanted to use more coal for the nation's energy needs. He also created the Department of Energy to try to solve the nation's energy problems.

The Camp David Accords

One of Jimmy Carter's most important accomplishments was promoting peace among the countries of the Middle East. Carter met with leaders from many of these countries. The most important of these meetings was held in September 1978 at Camp David, Maryland. Menachem Begin, from Israel, and Anwar Sadat, from Egypt, met with President Carter for two weeks. These meetings resulted in the Camp David Accords (agreements), leading to the signing of a peace treaty between Egypt and Israel on March 26, 1979.

President Carter, with Egyptian president Anwar Sadat and Israeli prime minister Menachem Begin, after signing the historic 1979 peace treaty between Egypt and Israel

President Jimmy Carter holds a town hall meeting
in Youngstown, Ohio, where he spent an hour
answering questions from the audience.

Carter wanted to stay in touch with his "boss"—the people of the United States. He was heard on radio talk shows and talked to people who called in to ask him questions. He attended town meetings and stayed overnight in people's homes. He listened to people's concerns and tried to find solutions to their problems.

Carter realized he could not accomplish all his goals. He focused on the most important issues. As president, he made progress on a new treaty transferring control of the Panama Canal to the people of Panama by 2000. He worked to make fair election laws, to reform the welfare system, and to create lasting peace in the Middle East.

Carter also participated in the second Strategic Arms Limitations Talks (SALT II) with the Soviet Union. A treaty was signed reducing the number of nuclear weapons in both countries. Jimmy led the fight for human rights throughout the world. He believed all people had the right to peace, environmental quality, democracy, and freedom.

**President Carter and Soviet President
Leonid Brezhnev sign the SALT II treaty.**

In 1980, Carter ran for reelection as president, but he was defeated by Ronald Reagan. When Carter left the presidency, there were many things he wished he had accomplished. Most of all, Carter wanted to bring home fifty-three Americans who had been held hostage in Iran for more than a year.

About four hundred Iranians seized the United States Embassy in Teheran, Iran, and captured fifty-three U.S. citizens on November 4, 1979. President Carter tried putting political and economic pressure on Iran, but the standoff continued for

34

**Some of the hostages taken in
the U.S. Embassy in Tehran, Iran**

444 days. The American hostages weren't released until January 20, 1981.

The hostages were released just after Reagan was sworn in as president. Carter was sorry that he couldn't be the one to announce their release to the nation. He was still happy they were able to come home to their families.

As a former president, Carter could have retired to the family home in Plains, Georgia, and spent his days relaxing in the sun. But he wanted to do more.

Sharing His Vision with the World

In 1982, Jimmy and Rosalynn founded the Carter Center of Emory University in Atlanta, Georgia. Jimmy Carter described it as "a place where people could come together to resolve their differences and solve problems." The center sponsors programs in democracy, human rights, and global health. It also operates economic and social development programs that try to improve the standard of living for people living in poor nations. Another mission for the center is to work

**Jimmy and Rosalynn Carter observe
elections in Indonesia in 1999.**

on inner-city problems in the United States.
The center's efforts reach out to people in about
sixty-five countries.

The Carter Center sends people to countries to
make sure that elections are run properly and legal-
ly. It also conducts peace missions in troubled countries around the world. The center works with the
Task Force for Child Survival and Development to

**During a trip to Zaire in 1995, Carter tried
to help find ways to resolve the Rwandan
and Burundian refugee crisis.**

rid the world of terrible diseases, such as guinea
worm disease and river blindness.

The Carter Center hopes to eliminate these
terrible diseases by the beginning of the twenty-
first century. Its programs have already
reduced the number of such cases by more than
ninety percent. The center has also helped

38

Terrible Diseases

Guinea worm disease comes from drinking impure water. The worms, or larvae, live inside the human body and can grow to a length of 3 feet (0.9 meters). When they emerge through the skin, it is painful and can cripple the victim.

River blindness is caused by a parasite that enters the human body through the bite of a blackfly. Symptoms include constant itching, skin rashes, and eye damage that sometimes leads to blindness.

increase worldwide immunizations against common childhood diseases, such as measles, chickenpox, and mumps.

Another Carter Center project, Global 2000, wants to end hunger in poor countries by teaching farmers better ways to grow crops on their land. The project provides improved seeds, fertilizer, and farming tools. In Ethiopia, farmers have tripled the amount of grain produced on their farms. For the first time in decades, they have extra food to trade with neighboring countries.

Carter works on a Habitat for Humanity project in New York in 1984.

The Atlanta Project is an attempt by the Carter Center to solve problems found in U.S. inner cities. The project's programs deal with crime and violence, unemployment, homelessness, and teenage pregnancy.

The Carter Center was not the only project Jimmy and Rosalynn became involved in after

Habitat for Humanity

Habitat for Humanity International was founded in 1976 by Millard and Linda Fuller. There are now more than 1,300 active local chapters of Habitat for Humanity in the United States and 250 international chapters. Using donations of cash and building supplies, and volunteers to do the work, Habitat for Humanity has built and improve more than 70,000 houses around the world.

he left the presidency. They'd always been concerned about homelessness. As a result, in 1984, Jimmy and Rosalynn became involved with Habitat for Humanity International, an organization whose goal is to build homes for families in need.

Every year, Jimmy and Rosalynn encourage support of Habitat for Humanity through their public-speaking engagements. In addition, they spend one week each year building houses with other Habitat volunteers.

Their involvement, called the Jimmy Carter Work Project (JCWP), is Habitat's most important annual event. The Carters' participation in the project helps to generate a lot of attention for Habitat and the plight of homeless people. In the third week of June 1998, volunteers at the JCWP, including the Carters, built one hundred new homes in Houston, Texas.

Since leaving office, Jimmy Carter has become known as "a tireless champion for social justice." People admire and respect the work he's done since leaving the White House. Jimmy has also written twelve books.

A reviewer of one of Jimmy Carter's books, *Turning Point*, sums up the feelings of most Americans about their thirty-ninth president: "Few individuals in our world today can match the achievements and moral stature of former President Jimmy Carter. It has been said, without exaggeration, that Jimmy Carter is the only man ever to have used the presidency as a stepping-stone to greater service."

Carter signs a copy of one of his books for an admirer.

In Your Community

You can help your friends find peaceful ways to settle any disagreements.

Jimmy Carter has devoted his life to peace and helping people in need. What can you do to help?

Disagreements with other people are a normal part of life. But when people disagree

Timeline

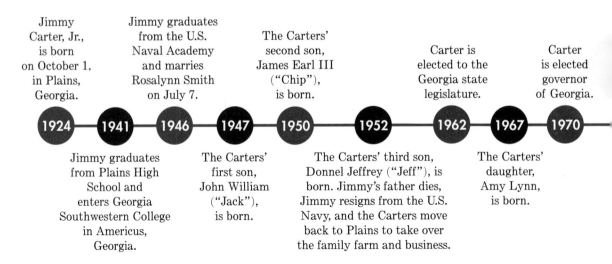

Jimmy Carter, Jr., is born on October 1, in Plains, Georgia.

Jimmy graduates from the U.S. Naval Academy and marries Rosalynn Smith on July 7.

The Carters' second son, James Earl III ("Chip"), is born.

Carter is elected to the Georgia state legislature.

Carter is elected governor of Georgia.

1924 — **1941** — **1946** — **1947** — **1950** — **1952** — **1962** — **1967** — **1970**

Jimmy graduates from Plains High School and enters Georgia Southwestern College in Americus, Georgia.

The Carters' first son, John William ("Jack"), is born.

The Carters' third son, Donnel Jeffrey ("Jeff"), is born. Jimmy's father dies, Jimmy resigns from the U.S. Navy, and the Carters move back to Plains to take over the family farm and business.

The Carters' daughter, Amy Lynn, is born.

they don't have to fight. Can you encourage your friends to resolve their arguments without fighting?

Can you volunteer to work with Habitat for Humanity and help build someone a new home? If not, you can still help raise money for Habitat projects. Find out if there is a local chapter of Habitat for Humanity in the community where you live. Call its office and ask how you can help. Jimmy Carter knows that helping others is the right thing to do, and it makes you feel great, too!

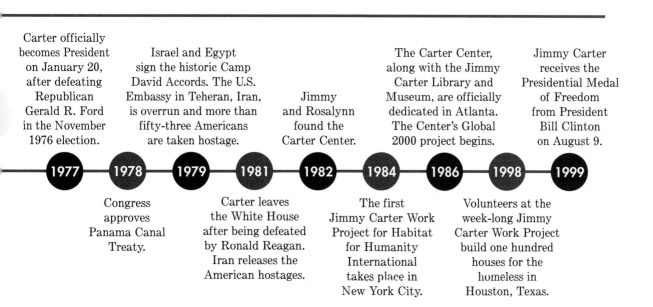

Carter officially becomes President on January 20, after defeating Republican Gerald R. Ford in the November 1976 election.

Israel and Egypt sign the historic Camp David Accords. The U.S. Embassy in Teheran, Iran, is overrun and more than fifty-three Americans are taken hostage.

Jimmy and Rosalynn found the Carter Center.

The Carter Center, along with the Jimmy Carter Library and Museum, are officially dedicated in Atlanta. The Center's Global 2000 project begins.

Jimmy Carter receives the Presidential Medal of Freedom from President Bill Clinton on August 9.

1977 — 1978 — 1979 — 1981 — 1982 — 1984 — 1986 — 1998 — 1999

Congress approves Panama Canal Treaty.

Carter leaves the White House after being defeated by Ronald Reagan. Iran releases the American hostages.

The first Jimmy Carter Work Project for Habitat for Humanity International takes place in New York City.

Volunteers at the week-long Jimmy Carter Work Project build one hundred houses for the homeless in Houston, Texas.

To Find Out More

Here are some additional resources to help you learn more about Jimmy Carter, the Carter Center, and Habitat for Humanity:

Books

Sandack, Cass R. *The Carters.* Crestwood House, 1993.

Schraff, Anne E. *Jimmy Carter.* Enslow Publishers, 1998.

Smith, Betsy Covington. *Jimmy Carter: President.* Walker & Co. Library, 1987.

Turk, Ruth. *Rosalynn Carter: Steel Magnolia.* Franklin Watts, 1997.

Wade, Linda R. *James Carter.* Children's Press, 1989.

Organizations and Online Sites

The Carter Center
One Copenhill Avenue
Atlanta, Georgia 30307
http://www.cartercenter.org

Jimmy Carter Presidential Library
441 Freedom Parkway
One Copenhill Avenue
Atlanta, Georgia 30307-1498
http://carterlibrary.galileo. peachnet.edu/

Habitat for Humanity International
121 Habitat Street
Americus, Georgia 31709-3498
http://www.habitat.org/

Jimmy Carter National Historic Site
300 N. Bond St.
Plains, Georgia 31780
http://www.nps.gov/jica/home.html

The White House
1600 Pennsylvania Avenue
Washington, D.C. 20500
http://www.whitehouse.gov/ WH/Welcome.html
Visit the White House where Jimmy Carter and his family lived during his presidency.

Index

About the Authors

Linda George earned her bachelor's degree in Elementary Education from the University of Texas at El Paso, in 1971. She taught in the elementary grades, every grade K–6, for ten years. She began her professional writing career in 1979, and writes for Harlequin/Silhouette as Madeline George.

Charles George earned his bachelor's degree in Spanish and History from Tarleton State University, Stephenville, Texas, in 1974. He taught Spanish and Advanced Social Studies for fifteen years on the high school level, then "retired" to write full time. He loves doing research.

Charles and Linda have authored more than two dozen non-fiction books for children and young adults, for Children's Press, the Cornerstones of Freedom, America the Beautiful and Community Builders series, Franklin Watts, Capstone Press, and Lucent Books.

They have been married since 1971, have two children, Christy and Alex, and live in Central Texas near the small town of Rising Star. They enjoy traveling in their travel trailer to do research and gather ideas for new projects.